Autumn ALPHABET

by jodie gerling

A is for APPLE

B is for BREEZE

i love you

TO THE MOON

and back

C is for CHILLY nights
before the first freeze.

D is for DEER

E is for EGGS

F is for FLANNEL
worn on cool autumn days.

G is for GOURDS

H is for HARVEST

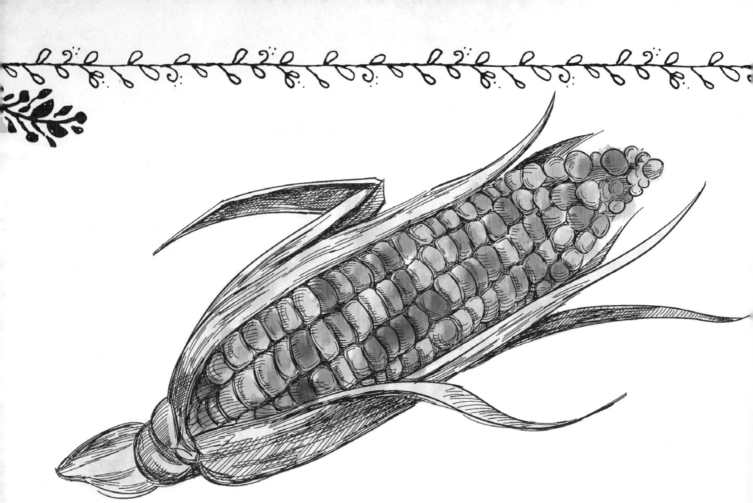

I is for INDIAN CORN
and I like it the best.

J is for JACK-O-LANTERN

K is for KIDS playing

L is for LEAVES falling,
and for leaf raking.

M is for MIGRATE

November

GIVE THANKS

N is for NOVEMBER

O is for OCTOBER
when there's a change in the weather.

P is for PUMPKIN PIE

Q is for QUILT

R is for RUSTLING leaves
near the campfire we built.

S is for SQUIRREL

T is for THANKSGIVING

U is for UMBRELLA
to keep us dry while it's raining.

V is for VIBRANT

W is for WOODLAND

X is for eXtra hot chocolate
warm in our hand.

Y is for YELLOW

Z is for ZIG-ZAGGING
and zipping through the leaf piles...

FRESH APPLE PIE

...while our apple pie
is baking.

Also By This Author

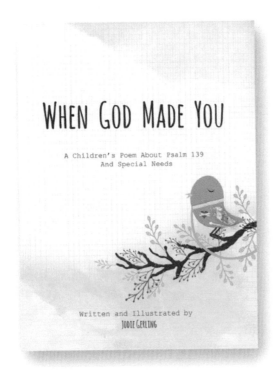

Available on Amazon.com
For more information about these books, please visit
www.mamaneedsquiettime.wordpress.com

69593251R00018